Vocabulary Workbook

PEARSON

Scott
Foresman

Editorial Offices: Glenview, Illinois • Parsippany, New Jersey • New York, New York
Sales Offices: Parsippany, New Jersey • Duluth, Georgia • Glenview, Illinois
Coppell, Texas • Ontario, California • Mesa, Arizona

www.sfsocialstudies.com

ISBN 0-328-09071-9

Copyright © Pearson Education, Inc.

8 9 10 V011 12 11 10 09 08 07

© Scott Foresman 6

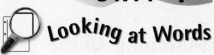

How Many Syllables?

It can be easier to read and spell new words, short or long, when you break them up into syllables. Remember, a syllable is a part of a word in which we hear a vowel sound. Here are some examples of how words can be broken into syllables:

- Break between double consonants. Example: *sum-mer*.
- Sometimes break between two different consonants. Example: *par-ty*.
- Sometimes a vowel stands alone. Example: *choc-o-late*.

For each word in the word box, determine the number of syllables. Then write each word in syllables on the lines below. Use a dictionary to check your work.

prehistory	archaeology	artifact	geography	domesticate
harvest	ziggurat	archaeologist	glacier	migrate
descendant	anthropology	technology	civilization	nomad
artisan	covenant	surplus	dynasty	agriculture

2 Syllables

_____

_____

_____

_____

3 Syllables

_____

_____

_____

_____

4 Syllables

_____

_____

_____

5 Syllables

_____

_____

_____

Notes for Home: Your child organized vocabulary words by the number of syllables in each word.
Home Activity: Have your child pronounce the remainder of the vocabulary words and tell how many syllables are in each word.

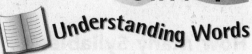

Understanding Words

Matching Game

Play this game with a partner. Each player needs a set of vocabulary cards on which is written his or her name.

Player 1: Stack all your vocabulary cards in a pile, word side up.

Player 2: Place all your vocabulary cards in a line, in any order, with the definition side up.

Player 1: Take the top card from the stack of cards with the word side up. Find the definition you feel matches the word. If the word and definition match, take the pair. If not, put the word card at the bottom of the stack and the definition card back in the line.

Player 2: Repeat the same steps as Player 1.

Keep playing by taking turns until there are no more cards to match. The player who has the most pairs at the end of the game is the winner.

Repeat the game until each player can match all the words and definitions. Then each player is a winner!

prehistory	archaeology	archaeologist	artifact
migrate	glacier	technology	domesticate
harvest	excavation site	agriculture	surplus
nomad	social division	climate	carbon dating
culture	anthropology	landform	geography
diverse	civilization	fertile	plain
plateau	irrigation	city-state	region
artisan	ziggurat	society	polytheism
scribe	cuneiform	conquer	empire
dynasty	conquest	covenant	monotheism
slavery	descendant	synagogue	barter

Notes for Home: Your child matched vocabulary words with definitions.
Home Activity: With your child, go over the words in this unit. Have him or her give you his or her own explanations of the words and then tell how they relate to the subjects of the unit.

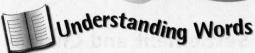

Words with -logy

The word part *-logy* means "study of" or "science of." The word part *zoo-* means "animal" or "animal kingdom." When you combine *-logy* with *zoo-* you get *zoology*, which means "the science concerned with the study of animals."

Read the definition for the opening word part of each of the vocabulary words below. Then write a definition for each vocabulary word based on your understanding of the word parts for each word.

1. archaeology: *archaeo-* means "ancient."

Definition: _____

2. technology: *techno-* means "technical."

Definition: _____

3. anthropology: *anthropo-* means "human being."

Definition: _____

Check your definitions of the words against the definitions on your vocabulary cards.

Now read the definitions of word parts in the box. Then write the answer to each question below by combining one of the word parts from the box with *-logy*.

bio-: living organisms	*ornitho-*: bird
geo-: earth	*socio-*: society

4. What word means a science that deals with birds?

_____

5. What word means the study of the earth through its rocks?

_____

6. What word means the study of organized groups of humans?

_____

7. What word means a science concerned with the study of living things?

_____

> **Notes for Home:** Your child used combined word parts to understand the meaning of vocabulary words and other words.
> **Home Activity:** Challenge your child to think of words with the word part *-graphy*, as in the vocabulary word **geography**. Have your child find the word parts for each word in a dictionary and compare their definitions to the definition of the whole word.

Name_____

Settlement and Change

Expository Writing

Between 10,000 and 3,000 years ago, life changed for people in North America. The development of agriculture allowed people to begin settling, rather than traveling from place to place in search of food. Think about what you have learned about the earliest settlements and how life changed. Write to explain how life changed when people began to settle. Use as many vocabulary words as possible. You may use an additional sheet of paper.

agriculture	artisan	barter	climate	conquer	culture
descendant	diverse	domesticate	fertile	geography	glacier
harvest	irrigation	landform	migrate	nomad	plain
plateau	region	social division	society	surplus	technology

_____

_____

_____

_____

_____

_____

_____

_____

_____

_____

_____

_____

_____

_____

_____

_____

 Notes for Home: Your child wrote an explanantion of how agriculture and the domestication of animals changed the way of life in prehistoric times.
Home Activity: Divide a sheet of paper into two columns labeled "Similarities" and "Differences." With your child, discuss and record the ways civilization today has changed or stayed the same compared to 50 years ago. Use the vocabulary words to spark discussion.

✂

prehistory	archaeology
archaeologist	artifact
migrate	glacier
technology	domesticate
harvest	

© Scott Foresman 6

the study of past cultures through the things that remain such as buildings, tools, or pottery

the long period of time before people developed systems of writing and written language

an object made by people long ago

a scientist who uncovers evidence, or proof, from the past

a huge ice sheet

to move from one place to another

to tame

the way in which humans produce the items they use

to gather

excavation site	**agriculture**
surplus	**nomad**
social division	**climate**
carbon dating	**culture**
anthropology	

© Scott Foresman 6

the raising of plants or animals for human use

a site where archaeologists uncover artifacts

a person who travels from place to place without a permanent home

an extra supply

the average weather conditions of a place over a long span of time

a group that does a certain type of work

the way in which individuals and groups react with their environment, including their technology, customs, beliefs, and art

a method of estimating the age of something after it has died

the study of how people have developed and live in cultural groups

landform	geography
diverse	civilization
fertile	plain
plateau	irrigation
city-state	

the study of the relationship between physical features, climate, and people

a natural feature of Earth's surface such as a valley, plain, hill, or mountain

a group of people who have a complex and organized society within a culture

different

an area of flat land

rich, as in soil

a system of transporting water to crops

an area of high, flat land

a city that is an individual unit, complete with its own form of government and traditions

region	artisan
ziggurat	society
polytheism	scribe
cuneiform	conquer
empire	

a craftsperson such as a potter or weaver

an area on Earth with common physical features

an organized community with established rules and traditions

a huge, pyramid-shaped structure consisting of a series of stacked, rectangular platforms

a professional writer

the worship of many gods

to defeat

a form of wedge-shaped writing used in ancient times

a large territory consisting of many different places under the control of a single ruler

dynasty	conquest
covenant	monotheism
slavery	descendant
synagogue	barter

the defeat of another group

a ruling family

the worship of only one God

an agreement

a person born later into the same family

the practice of one person owning another person

to exchange one kind of good or service for another

a Jewish place of worship

Plurals of Compound Nouns

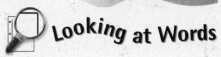
Looking at Words

The three types of compound words are closed *(classmate)*, open *(high school)*, and hyphenated *(left-handed)*.

Most compound nouns are made plural by adding *s* or *es*, or by dropping *y* and adding *ies*.

    seat belt/seat belts   toothbrush/toothbrushes   blueberry/blueberries

For hyphenated compound nouns, make the most important word plural:

    mother-in-law/mothers-in-law   great-aunt/great-aunts

Do not forget irregular plurals:

    grandchild/grandchildren   field mouse/field mice

Circle the correct plural form of each vocabulary word below.

1. **oracle bone:**   oracles bone   oracle bons   oracle bones

2. **middleman:**   middlemans   middlemen   middlesmen

3. **monsoon season:**   monsoons seasons   monsoon seasons   monsoons season

For each compound noun below, write its plural form on the blank line below it. Use a dictionary to check your answers.

4. dining room

5. father-in-law

6. lunchroom

7. drive-in

8. textbook

9. chairwoman

10. cough drop

11. motorcycle

12. stepchild

13. half-dollar

14. penalty box

15. crybaby

Notes for Home: Your child practiced finding and writing plurals of compound nouns. **Home Activity:** Have your child write the plurals of household objects that are compound nouns, such as *desktop* or *bookcase*.

Name_____

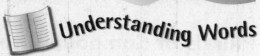

Understanding Words

Crack the Code

The vocabulary word **pictograph** is a combination of two word parts. The part *picto* means "have painted" and *-graph* means "something written or drawn." The word **pictograph** means "a picture that represents a word in a writing system."

Many other words are built with the word part *-graph*. To find some of these words, read the clues and use the code key. Write the missing word part for each word in the space provided. Then use a dictionary to find the definition of each word and write it on the blank line.

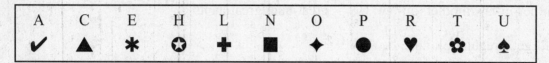

A	C	E	H	L	N	O	P	R	T	U
✔	▲	✳	✪	✚	■	◆	●	♥	✿	♠

1. Say "cheese" when this is taken.

 graph

Definition: _____

2. Dad still plays old records on this.

● ✪ ◆ ■ ◆ graph

Definition: _____

3. This is the way to dance.

 graph

Definition: _____

4. Please sign right here.

✔ ♠ ✿ ◆ graph

Definition: _____

5. There's a message in the wire.

 graph

Definition: _____

 Notes for Home: Your child cracked a code to build words with the word part *-graph*.
Home Activity: The word *telegraph* begins with the word part *tele-*. Ask your child to make a list of other words that begin with *tele-*, such as *television*. Have your child look up the meaning of *tele-* and each word in a dictionary.

Vocabulary Workbook

Twenty Questions

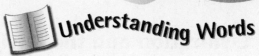

Understanding Words

Work with a partner. Use one set of vocabulary cards. Place all of the cards in a container. Player 1 draws a card and holds it so Player 2 cannot see it. Player 2 can ask twenty "yes" or "no" questions to try to figure out what vocabulary word Player 1 is holding. Players switch roles each time.

As you play, be sure to tally the number of questions you ask. When you have guessed the word, or asked all twenty questions, write down the word in the blank and the number of questions it took to guess it. If you were unable to guess the word, your score for that word is 25.

When each player has guessed five words, add up the total number of questions you asked. The player who asked the least number of questions is the winner.

Player 1

Word	Questions
1.	
2.	
3.	
4.	
5.	
Total	

Player 2

Word	Questions
1.	
2.	
3.	
4.	
5.	
Total	

Notes for Home: Today your child reviewed the meanings of the vocabulary words by playing a guessing game with a partner.
Home Activity: Work with your child to search the Internet and reference books to find images of the ten vocabulary words listed on this page. Have your child comment on each image by telling what he or she knows after reading the unit.

Civilization and the Environment

Expository Writing

The environment of a place affects the ways of life developed by people who live in that place. The environment of Egypt is unique. Think about how the environment may have affected the ways of life Egyptians developed, such as agricultural methods and cultural practices. Write to explain the ways in which the ancient civilization of Egypt interacted with the environment. Use as many vocabulary words as possible. You may use an additional sheet of paper.

cataract	delta	economy	silt	unify	mummy
papyrus	hieroglyphics	independent	pharaoh	pyramid	

_____

_____

_____

_____

_____

_____

_____

_____

_____

_____

_____

_____

_____

_____

_____

_____

_____

_____

Notes for Home: Your child wrote about the ways the civilization of ancient Egypt interacted with its environment.

Home Activity: Discuss with your child how environmental factors (such as landforms, water, climate, and natural resources) affect daily life in your city, town, or region of the country.

delta

silt

papyrus

cataract

unify

pharaoh

hieroglyphics

pyramid

a mixture of soil and small rocks

a triangular-shaped area at the mouth of some rivers

waterfall

a plant whose stems are used to make a kind of paper

in ancient Egypt, a god-king

to unite, combine, or bring together

a large stone building to serve as a house for the dead

a form of writing based on pictures

mummy

economy

independent

loess

terrace

levee

double cropping

pictograph

the way people use and manage resources

a preserved dead body

a yellowish brown soil that blows in from a desert

free

a dike used to control flooding

a platform of earth

a picture that represents a word

a process in which two crops are grown on the same land in the same year

© Scott Foresman 6

oracle bone

province

ancestor

civil service

middleman

nobility

subcontinent

monsoon season

political division

a bone commonly used during the Shang dynasty in China to predict the future

the practice of using skills and talents to work in the government

a relative who lived longer ago than a grandparent

a high-ranking social class

a person who goes between buyers and sellers

rainy season in monsoon climates in which winds blow from the southwest for six months

a large area of land that is separated by water from other lands

subsistence farming

Brahmin

sudra

reincarnation

caste

meditation

enlightenment

a priest who held the highest position in Aryan society	the process of growing food mainly for self-consumption
the Hindu belief that the spirit or soul goes from one life to the next	a serf in Hindu society
in Buddhism, a way of clearing the mind	in Hinduism, a lifelong social group into which one is born
	in Buddhism, a state of pure goodness, the goal of reincarnation

Name_____

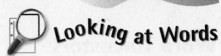
Guide Words

Words in a dictionary are arranged in alphabetical order. Guide words at the top of each page help you to find words quickly, because they tell you the first and last words on each page. Write each vocabulary word from the word box in alphabetical order on a blank line below the guide words it falls between.

peninsula	cenote	theocracy	aqueduct	codex	mercenary
causeway	alliance	wetland	biome	archipelago	quipu
tributary	tundra	arid	etching	pueblo	adobe
wattle	wigwam	snowhouse			

actual–almanac

_____

_____

cobble–cog

_____

_____

pry–quit

_____

_____

aquatic–army

_____

_____

_____

estuary–ethics

_____

_____

_____

snail–there

_____

_____

_____

bicycle–binary

_____

_____

mention–merchant

_____

_____

trial–tunnel

_____

_____

_____

catwalk–century

_____

_____

palace–people

_____

_____

waffle–will

_____

_____

 Notes for Home: Today your child arranged vocabulary words in alphabetical order by using guide words.
Home Activity: Have your child find last names or business names in your local telephone directory by using guide words.

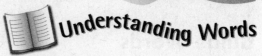

Word Ancestors

Just as people are descended from ancestors who lived long ago, many words we use today are descended from words used in ancient Latin and Greek. Write the vocabulary word that comes from each word origin listed below. Then write a brief description of how the modern word is related in meaning to the Latin or Greek word. Use your vocabulary cards or a dictionary to help you remember the modern definitions.

aqueduct	**archipelago**	**arid**	**biome**
mercenary	**peninsula**	**theocracy**	**tributary**

Latin Word Origins

tribuere (to assign) ____tributary____

A tributary is "assigned" to a larger stream, because it flows into it._____

1. *merces* (wages) _____

_____

2. *aquae* + *ductus* (water + act of leading) _____

_____

3. *paene* + *insula* (almost + an island) _____

_____

4. *aridus* (dry) _____

_____

Greek Word Origins

5. *theo* + *-kratia* (God + strength, power, or rule) _____

_____

6. *archi-* + *pelagos* (rule + sea) _____

_____

7. *bios* (life) _____

_____

 Notes for Home: Your child learned about Latin and Greek word origins.
Home Activity: Have your child use the Latin and Greek word origins they have learned to brainstorm a list of other words.

Name_____

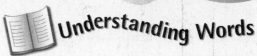

What Would You Do?

Understanding Words

Use your understanding of the vocabulary words to answer the following questions. Be sure to explain your reasoning.

1. Would you be more likely to open a vacation resort on **tundra** or on an **archipelago**? Why?

_____

_____

_____

2. If you usually prefer to be alone, would you live in a **longhouse** or a **wigwam**? Why?

_____

_____

_____

3. Would you record your predictions of the future in a **codex** or a **quipu**? Why?

_____

_____

_____

4. Would you cross water on a **causeway** or a **chinampa**? Why?

_____

_____

_____

5. Which would you find in nature, a **tributary** or an **aqueduct**? Why?

_____

_____

_____

6. To visit an **arid** climate, would you go to a **scrub land** or a **wetland**? Why?

_____

_____

_____

 Notes for Home: Your child demonstrated his or her understanding of vocabulary words by answering questions.
Home Activity: Have your child create his or her own questions using the vocabulary words for this unit.

The Greatest Civilization

Persuasive Writing

The civilizations of Mesoamerica—the Olmec, the Maya, and the Aztec—were all powerful and made significant advances in science, culture, and technology. Think about the different developments each civilization made. Write to persuade someone about which Mesoamerican civilization you think made the greatest contributions. Use as many vocabulary words as possible. You may use an additional sheet of paper.

adobe	alliance	aqueduct	mercenary	causeway
cenote	chinampa	codex	peninsula	theocracy

_____

_____

_____

_____

_____

_____

_____

_____

_____

_____

_____

_____

_____

_____

_____

_____

_____

_____

_____

 Notes for Home: Your child wrote about a Mesoamerican civilization.
Home Activity: Have your child read his or her persuasive argument aloud. Together, discuss the points made.

peninsula	cenote
theocracy	aqueduct
codex	mercenary
chinampa	causeway

natural wells on the Yucatán Peninsula

land that is nearly surrounded by water

structures used to carry flowing water from a distance

a system of government in which the rulers are believed to represent the will of the gods

a hired soldier

a folding-screen book containing information about predicting the future and religious rituals

raised bridges made of land

man-made island

✂

alliance	**wetland**
biome	**scrub land**
archipelago	**quipu**
basin and range	

land that is covered with moist soil

an agreement made between two or more groups or nations

an area of low-growing vegetation

a place that has a distinct climate, plants, and animals

a knotted rope used by the Incas to keep records

a close group of islands

a low area of land with a small mountain range

tributary

tundra

arid

etching

pit house

pueblo

adobe

flat area where trees cannot grow

a small stream that flows into a larger stream or river

an imprinted drawing or design

dry

a structure of adobe brick

a dwelling used by the Hohokam and made from digging a hole in the ground and covering it with logs

a brick formed from mud and straw that is dried in the sun

✂

burial mound	wattle
wigwam	temple mound
snowhouse	sod house
longhouse	

a wall material made from branches and vines intertwined with logs

a small hill of dirt built over the grave of a person

hill of dirt built for ceremonies

a dome-shaped hut made of branches covered with animal skins or woven mats

a shelter made from blocks of earth

a house of snow blocks used by the Inuit

a large, rectangular building used by the Iroquois that housed many families

Name_____

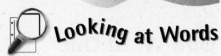

Break It Up

It can be easier to read and spell new words, short or long, when you break them up into syllables. Remember, a syllable is a part of a word in which we hear a vowel sound. For each word in the word box, determine the number of syllables. Then write each word in syllables on the lines below. Use a dictionary to check your work.

agora	aristocracy	Caesar	catacomb	consul
democracy	dictator	disciple	emperor	gladiator
immortal	marathon	mercenary	patrician	patriotism
persecute	philosopher	pillage	plebeian	plunder
reason	representative	republic	Senate	synagogue
tribune	vandal			

2 Syllables

_____   _____   _____

_____   _____   _____

_____   _____   _____

3 Syllables

_____   _____   _____

_____   _____   _____

_____   _____   _____

4 Syllables   ## 5 Syllables

_____   _____

_____   _____

_____

Notes for Home: Your child practiced breaking up vocabulary words into syllables.
Home Activity: Together with your child, look up some of the vocabulary words in the dictionary. Notice where the syllable breaks and stresses are placed.

Name_____

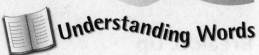
Odd Word Out

Circle the word that does not belong with the others. Explain your choice. Include a description of how the other three words are related in meaning. Use the vocabulary cards to help you.

1. **plunder**   **pillage**   **vandalize**   **protect**

_____

_____

_____

2. **consul**   **representative**   **gladiator**   **tribune**

_____

_____

_____

3. **democracy**   **aristocracy**   **nobility**   **patrician**

_____

_____

_____

4. **emperor**   **caesar**   **dictator**   **philosopher**

_____

_____

_____

 Notes for Home: Your child found similarities in meaning among vocabulary words.
Home Activity: Discuss with your child the differences in meanings for the individual words within the groups of similar words in this activity.

Vocabulary Workbook

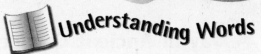

Suffixes -er and -or

Understanding Words

When you add a suffix to a root word, you change the meaning of the word. Each of the three vocabulary words in the first row of the word box has the suffix *-er* or *-or*. The suffixes *-er* and *-or* mean "a person who does something" or "a person who is connected to something."

emperor	dictator	philosopher	senate
marathon	reason	persecute	

Each definition below contains a root word for one of the three vocabulary words that end in *-er* or *-or*. Write the vocabulary word on the line next to its definition.

1. a person with the power to dictate _____

2. a person who studies philosophy _____

3. the head of an empire _____

Now look at the other four vocabulary words. Use a dictionary to find out how to add *-er* or *-or* to each word. Write each new word and its definition in the space provided.

Root Word	New Word	Definition
4. senate	_____	_____
5. marathon	_____	_____
6. reason	_____	_____
7. persecute	_____	_____

List other words with *-er* or *-or* and their roots below. An example has been completed for you.

A person who _____writes_____ is a _____writer_____.

8. A person who _____ is a _____.

9. A person who _____ is a _____.

10. A person who _____ is a _____.

11. A person who _____ is a _____.

Notes for Home: Your child learned the meanings of vocabulary words by using the suffixes *-er* and *-or*.
Home Activity: Discuss with your child different occupations with names that have the suffix *-er* or *-or*. Have your child find the root words in a dictionary and tell you their definitions.

A Day in Ancient Greece

Narrative Writing

Education was an extremely important part of life in ancient Greece. Suppose you are a student in ancient Greece. Write a journal entry describing the events of your day, the people you meet, and the new subjects and ideas that you are studying. Use at least four vocabulary words. You may use an additional sheet of paper.

agora	aristocracy	democracy	immortal	marathon	myth
mercenary	plunder	philosopher	plague	reason	

_____

_____

_____

_____

_____

_____

_____

_____

_____

_____

_____

_____

_____

_____

_____

_____

_____

_____

_____

_____

_____

 Notes for Home: Your child wrote about a day in the life of a student in ancient Greece.
Home Activity: Ask your child to describe to you what life was like in the ancient civilizations of Greece and Rome. Try to find images of these civilizations in books or on the Internet.

agora	plunder
myth	**immortal**
aristocracy	**democracy**
marathon	**philosopher**

valuables taken in war

an outdoor marketplace in
ancient Greece

to live forever

a traditional story that may include gods
and goddesses and often tries to explain
events in nature

a government by the people

a government controlled by a few
wealthy people

a person who studies truth
and knowledge

the longest race in the Olympics,
a footrace of about 26 miles

reason

plague

mercenary

patrician

plebeian

republic

representative

Senate

an epidemic of an often fatal disease	logical thinking
a wealthy, powerful citizen of ancient Rome	a hired soldier
a form of government in which citizens have the right to choose their leaders	a common citizen of ancient Rome
a governing body in which ancient Roman representatives served	a person elected to represent the people

✂

consul	dictator
tribune	**patriotism**
Caesar	**emperor**
gladiator	**catacomb**

Name_____

a person who has total control over the people	in ancient Rome, one of two officials who managed the government and the army
a sense of pride in one's country	in ancient Rome, men who were appointed to protect the rights of plebeians
the ruler of an empire	an ancient Roman emperor
an underground room used as a burial site	in ancient Rome, a professional fighter

synagogue	disciple
persecute	auction
Pope	pillage
vandal	

one of a small group of people who followed Jesus

a Jewish place of worship

to sell something to the highest bidder

to punish

to rob

the leader of the Roman Catholic Church

a person who destroys property

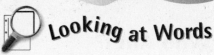

Middle English

When you read about the Middle Ages in Unit 5, did you think people in Britain spoke and wrote English the way we do today? Chaucer was a poet who wrote toward the end of the Middle Ages, between A.D. 1300 and 1400. Look at the excerpt below from his poem "The Canterbury Tales," which is about people setting out on a journey to a shrine in Canterbury, England. Many words may look unfamiliar. Now read the lines aloud. Can you recognize words from the way they sound? Do you recognize two of the vocabulary words from this unit, even though they are spelled differently today?

1. Write the modern spelling of the boldfaced words on the lines in the modern English translation. Use your vocabulary cards to help you.

Middle English

A **knyght** ther was, and that a worthy man,

That fro the tyme that he first bigan

To riden out, he loved **chivalrie,**

Trouthe and honour, fredom and curteisie.

Modern English

A _____ there was, and he a worthy man,

That from the time that he first began

To ride out, he loved _____,

Truth and honor, freedom and courtesy.

2. Now read the story that follows. The boldfaced words are from Middle English and are old versions of some vocabulary words. "Translate" each word into modern English. Write each correct vocabulary word in order on the lines below the story. Again, you may use your vocabulary cards if you need help.

On the Old Mill Road

On a **pilgrymage** to Canterbury, I traveled down the Old Mill Road. This path brought me past an ancient **covent**, and, as it was becoming dark outside, I stopped and knocked on the door. Many minutes later an old **nonne**, all dressed in black, answered the door. I asked if I might find some lodging. The elderly woman replied that no men could stay within those walls, but that I might try the **monasterie** about five miles down the road. Well, I thanked her for her time and set off to find the monks. Ah, if only my fellow merchants in the **gilde** could see me now, I thought. All alone and without a roof to call my own!

pilgrymage _____   monasterie _____

covent _____   gilde _____

nonne _____

Notes for Home: Your child compared the spelling of some of this unit's vocabulary words to their Middle English counterparts.
Home Activity: Read the Middle English version of the poem aloud together with your child. Discuss together what the poem says about the knight.

Name_____

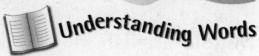

Who Am I?

Play with a partner. Find all the unit vocabulary cards that are listed in the word box. Shuffle and stack the cards. Player 1 draws a card. Player 2 must ask no more than ten "yes" or "no" questions to find out Player 1's identity. If Player 2 names the correct identity, he or she keeps the card. If not, the card goes back in the deck. Take turns until the deck is emptied. The player with the most cards wins. Each player should write the words and brief definitions on the lines below.

| shogun | monk | lady | daimyo | nun | serf |
| aristocrat | oba | samurai | knight | missionary | griot |

Identity: _____   Identity: _____

Definition: _____   Definition: _____

_____   _____

Identity: _____   Identity: _____

Definition: _____   Definition: _____

_____   _____

Identity: _____   Identity: _____

Definition: _____   Definition: _____

_____   _____

Identity: _____   Identity: _____

Definition: _____   Definition: _____

_____   _____

Identity: _____   Identity: _____

Definition: _____   Definition: _____

_____   _____

Identity: _____   Identity: _____

Definition: _____   Definition: _____

_____   _____

 Notes for Home: Your child played a game to reinforce the meanings of vocabulary words about the world during the Middle Ages.
Home Activity: Ask your child to explain the roles of these people within the different cultures he or she has learned about.

© Scott Foresman 6

Analogy Completion

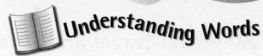
Understanding Words

An analogy is one way to show relationships between words. Use each word in the word box once to complete the analogies. Then write a sentence explaining why the relationship between the two sets of words is the same.

> cathedral   convent   knight   monarch   mosque
> nun   typhoon

Example: *juice* is to *glass* as

       soup is to _____bowl_____

       Why? _Juice is served in a glass, and soup is served in a bowl._____

1. *hurricane* is to *Atlantic* as

_____ is to *Pacific*

Why? _____

_____

2. *sportsmanship* is to *ballplayer* as

chivalry is to _____

Why? _____

_____

3. *oba* is to _____ as

samurai is to *soldier*

Why? _____

_____

4. *monk* is to *monastery* as

_____ is to _____

Why? _____

_____

5. _____ is to *Christians* as

_____ is to *Muslims*

Why? _____

_____

>
> **Notes for Home:** Today your child used vocabulary words to complete analogies.
> **Home Activity:** Have your child make analogies for words he or she knows. Ask your child to explain each analogy to you.

Medieval Travel and Trade
Narrative Writing

The Middle Ages were a time of increased travel and international trade. Ideas as well as valuable goods moved between continents. Suppose you are a trader who has returned from a successful trip across Europe, Africa, or Asia. Describe your travels in a brief report for the local paper, telling where you have been, who you met, the things you saw and learned, and what you brought back. Include as many vocabulary words as possible from the list. You may use an additional sheet of paper.

chivalry	convent	epidemic	guild	icon	knight
lady	missionary	monarch	monastery	monk	mosque
nun	pilgrimage	caravan	Swahili	serf	

_____

_____

_____

_____

_____

_____

_____

_____

_____

_____

_____

_____

_____

_____

_____

_____

_____

_____

Notes for Home: Today your child wrote about travel and trade in the Middle Ages.
Home Activity: Ask your child to tell you about the sights, experiences, people, and places described in his or her narrative. Use a map to locate the places mentioned.

Vocabulary Workbook

hippodrome	**cathedral**
icon	**pilgrimage**
caravan	**mosque**
astrolabe	**aristocrat**
samurai	**typhoon**

a large, important Christian church

an ancient Greek stadium used for horse and chariot racing

a journey to a place of religious importance

a religious image

a Muslim place of worship

a group of people and animals traveling together

a person who is a member of a high social class

an instrument used by navigators

a tropical storm with heavy winds and rough seas

a member of the Japanese warrior class

daimyo	shogun
savanna	griot
Swahili	oba
monk	nun
monastery	

a high-ranking military commander in Japan

a powerful samurai who controlled many other samurai and governed large areas of farmland in Japan

a professional storyteller from Africa

a short grassy plain

a king of Benin

a culture and language that combines African and Arabic cultures and languages

a woman who devotes her life to religion and lives in a convent

a man who devotes his life to religion and lives in a monastery

a community where monks live, study, and pray

convent

missionary

monarch

serf

knight

chivalry

guild

lady

epidemic

a person who teaches a religion to people with different beliefs

a community of nuns

a person who lived on and farmed feudal land

a king or queen who is a supreme leader

a knight's code of behavior

a feudal warrior trained and prepared to fight on horseback

a woman of nobility

a group of craftspeople or merchants who are united by a common interest

a disease that spreads quickly

Name_____

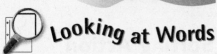

Adding a Suffix

Looking at Words

The suffixes *-al, -ial,* and *-ile* mean "of," or "pertaining to." Adding one of these suffixes to a root word creates the adjective form of the word:

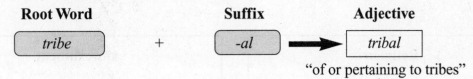

Root Word	Suffix	Adjective
tribe	+ -al →	tribal

"of or pertaining to tribes"

The suffix *-ism* means "belief in," "practice of," "system of," or "condition of." Adding *-ism* to the adjective form of a word creates a new noun:

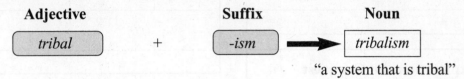

Adjective	Suffix	Noun
tribal	+ -ism →	tribalism

"a system that is tribal"

Add suffixes to the root words below to create new words. For many words, the spelling will change when you add suffixes. You may use a dictionary and your vocabulary cards to help.

Root Word	Adjective Form	Noun Form
	(Modify spelling and add *-al, -ial,* or *-ile.*)	(Add *-ism.*)
1. colony: a settlement that is far from its ruling nation	_____	_____
2. commerce: the large-scale selling and buying of goods	_____	_____
3. merchant: someone who makes a living by buying and selling goods	_____	_____
4. nation: a populated territory that is usually large and independent	_____	_____
5. empire: a huge territory of different peoples ruled by one authority	_____	_____
6. industry: an area's whole activity of manufacturing	_____	_____

Notes for Home: Today your child learned to create new forms of words by adding suffixes.
Home Activity: Together with your child, brainstorm a list of words that end with the suffix *-ism.*

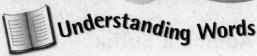

Understanding Words

Sorting Action

Sort your vocabulary cards into the categories listed below. Write the vocabulary words that belong under each heading.

Religion

_____

_____

Government

_____

_____

_____

Exploration and Conquest

_____

_____

_____

_____

_____

_____

_____

Social Movements

_____

_____

_____

Industry

_____

_____

_____

_____

Notes for Home: Your child organized this unit's vocabulary words into five basic categories to reinforce meanings.
Home Activity: Invite your child to brainstorm other words for each of the five categories.

Word Family Trees

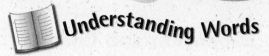Understanding Words

Word families are groups of words that share the same root. For example, *telephone,* *microphone,* and *phonograph* all share the same root *phon* or *phono,* which means "sound" or "voice."

When you know the root of a word and the origin of the root, you can predict the meaning of other words in the same family. For example, you may predict that the word *phonic* means "having to do with sound."

Below are explanations for four Latin roots that are a part of some of the words from this unit. Use them to help you match the words below to their definitions. Once you have matched, underline the root as you see it in the words. Then, circle the part of the definition that indicates its root.

circum	*legis*	*factor*	*corp*
Origin: *circus* (Latin)	Origin: *lex* (Latin)	Origin: *facere* (Latin)	Origin: *corpus* (Latin)
Meaning: circle	Meaning: law	Meaning: do or make	Meaning: body

1. ___k___ legal

2. _____ **legislature**

3. _____ manufacture

4. _____ **circumnavigate**

5. _____ circus

6. _____ corpse

7. _____ legitimate

8. _____ **corporation**

9. _____ circumference

10. _____ artifact

11. _____ **factory**

12. _____ incorporate

a. to make by hand or by machine

b. acceptable; admitted by law

c. a place where people and machines do work to make things

d. a dead human body

e. to make one thing a part of something else, as if one body

f. anything made by human skill or work

g. to circle the globe

h. an organization that may legally act as a single body

i. a show with different acts in a circle or ring

j. a group of representatives who make laws

k. according to law

l. the boundary line of a circle

Notes for Home: Your child used word roots and origins to predict the meaning of words in word families.
Home Activity: Challenge your child to think of words in the word family for the root *photo,* from the Greek word *phos,* which means "light." Have your child write a definition for each word and check the definitions in a dictionary.

Expansion and Change
Expository Writing

Beginning in the late 1400s and early 1500s, nations began to expand their trade routes, establish colonies, and spread their cultures into new lands. By the 1600s and 1700s, new nations were growing out of those colonies. Write to explain either the way in which a country expanded its influence over a colony or how a new nation developed during this time period. Use at least three vocabulary words. You may use an additional sheet of paper.

circumnavigate	colony	commerce	compound	conquistador
dominion	imperialism	imperialist	legislature	mercantilism
nationalism	treaty port			

_____

_____

_____

_____

_____

_____

_____

_____

_____

_____

_____

_____

_____

_____

_____

_____

_____

_____

_____

_____

Notes for Home: Today your child wrote about expansion, colonization, and the development of nations from the 1400s through the 1700s.
Home Activity: Discuss with your child ways in which trade is expanded or how nations change today. You may also wish to discuss types of exploration that still take place.

Vocabulary Workbook

commerce	**indulgence**
excommunicate	**circumnavigate**
conquistador	**colony**
mercantilism	**legislature**

© Scott Foresman 6

in the Roman Catholic Church,
a pardon for sin

the buying and selling of a large
quantity of goods

to travel around the world

to expel from a church

a settlement far from the country
that governs

a Spanish conqueror

a group of elected people who
make laws

a system in which a country uses its
colonies to obtain raw materials, makes
products from the raw materials, and
then sells the goods back to the colonists

massacre

monarchy

textile

factory

tenement

corporation

reformer

strike

government in which a king, queen, or emperor has supreme power

the killing of many helpless people

a building that houses many machines

cloth that is either woven or knitted

a business organization

an overcrowded slum apartment building

the refusal to work until demands are met

a person who tries to change or improve something

nationalism

imperialism

imperialist

treaty port

compound

modernization

dominion

parliament

a system of building an empire by conquering lands around the world

a strong devotion to one's country

Asian port cities that were open to trade with Western countries

a person who promotes imperialism

the process of bringing ways and standards to those of the present

a set-aside area

an elected legislature

a self-governing nation with strong ties to a ruling empire

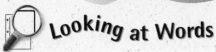
Looking at Words

The Right Suffix

You can build a noun from a verb by adding the suffix *-ion* or the suffix *-ment*.

Verb		**Suffix**		**Noun**

confuse	+	-ion	→	confusion
"to mix up"		"act of," "condition of being," or "result of"		"the condition of being mixed up"

advance	+	-ment	→	advancement
"to move forward"		"process of," "fact of," or "product or result of"		"the process of moving forward"

For each sentence below, the base word needed to complete the sentence is given. Complete each sentence by adding *-ion* or *-ment* to the base word and writing the new word on the blank line. Use your vocabulary cards to help you complete the first five sentences. For the rest of the sentences, use a dictionary.

1. *depress:* Many people were unemployed during the last _____.

2. *inflate:* _____ led to a sharp increase in the price of gasoline.

3. *contain:* The United States used a policy of _____ to fight communism.

4. *concentrate:* Nazis used the _____ camp as a method of getting rid of innocent people.

5. *appease:* Great Britain at first used _____ in dealing with Adolf Hitler.

6. *embarrass:* Her _____ at her mistake made her hide her face.

7. *educate:* To get a good job, you need a good _____.

8. *argue:* The two brothers disagreed and had a loud _____.

9. *measure:* They took a _____ of the floor space before buying a new rug.

10. *complete:* The team was given a trophy after _____ of the game.

Notes for Home: Your child built words by choosing the suffixes *-ion* and *-ment*.
Home Activity: Have your child read a chapter of a historical novel and make a list of the words with suffixes. Challenge your child to identify each base word.

Name_____

Word Family Sentences

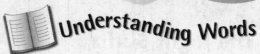Understanding Words

Within the same word family, there can be nouns, adjectives, verbs, and other parts of speech. Show your knowledge of parts of speech by writing a sentence for each word in each group. Use a dictionary to help you with unfamiliar words.

1. mobilize (verb), mobile (adjective), **mobilization** (noun)

_____

_____

_____

2. repair (verb), repairable (adjective), **reparation** (noun)

_____

_____

_____

3. inflate (verb), inflatable (adjective), **inflation** (noun)

_____

_____

_____

4. depress (verb), depressible (adjective), **depression** (noun)

_____

_____

_____

5. concentrate (verb), concentric (adjective), **concentration** (noun)

_____

_____

_____

6. aggressor (noun), aggressive (adjective), **aggression** (noun)

_____

_____

_____

 Notes for Home: Your child demonstrated his or her understanding of the parts of speech using words related to this unit's vocabulary words.
Home Activity: Ask your child to name the part of speech (noun, verb, or adjective) for each word on this page. Use a dictionary for help if needed.

A Turbulent Century

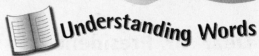

Understanding Words

Sort the vocabulary cards for the 20 vocabulary words in the word box into three categories based on when they are introduced in the unit: The Great War (WWI), World War II, and The Cold War. Write the words for each category on the lines below. Review the unit if you need help in sorting.

fascism	holocaust	refugee	trench warfare
neutral	propaganda	proletarian	annex
détente	casualty	reparations	mobilization
guerilla	nuclear	aggression	concentration camp
Nazis	containment	armistice	appeasement

The Great War (WWI)

_____   _____

_____   _____

_____   _____

_____

World War II

_____   _____

_____   _____

_____   _____

_____

The Cold War

_____   _____

_____   _____

_____

Notes for Home: Your child sorted the vocabulary cards for this unit into three thematic categories, and played a game using those categories.
Home Activity: Your child sorted the vocabulary words based on their introduction in the unit. Point out that many of the words, such as *holocaust,* are also relevant to other periods. You may want to help your child search for the words on the Internet to see their application throughout history.

Dear Mr. President
Persuasive Writing

By 1941 Great Britain was still fighting against Germany. Suppose you are a close adviser to British Prime Minister Winston Churchill, who has asked you to try to get the support of the United States. Think about what issues might cause the United States to consider joining the side of Great Britain. Write a letter to persuade President Franklin D. Roosevelt to have the United States enter World War II. Use at least five of the vocabulary words. You may use an additional sheet of paper.

aggression	annex	appeasement	fascism	concentration camp
Nazis	mobilization	propaganda	neutral	

_____

_____

_____

_____

_____

_____

_____

_____

_____

_____

_____

_____

_____

_____

_____

_____

_____

Notes for Home: Your child wrote a persuasive letter arguing for U.S. involvement in World War II.
Home Activity: Have your child create a time line based on what he or she has written in the activity.

mobilization

neutral

casualty

trench warfare

armistice

holocaust

reparations

inflation

one that does not take sides

the preparations nations make before sending their armies into battle

the use of deep ditches to shelter troops in battle

a wounded or killed soldier

a mass killing

a cease-fire

a rapid increase in prices

a payment for war losses

depression

fascism

Nazis

propaganda

aggression

annex

appeasement

collective

a form of government that stresses the
nation above individuals

a period of sharp economic decline

the planned spread of certain beliefs

the National Socialists, Germany's
former fascist party

to attach or to add

a policy of launching attacks on
the territory of others

farms that are grouped together and
run by the government

to preserve peace by meeting the
demands of an aggressor

refugee	**concentration camp**
charter	**nuclear**
containment	**proletarian**
guerrilla	**détente**

a place that holds imprisoned people of a particular ethnic group for their political or religious beliefs

a person who leaves his or her homeland for a safer place

atomic

a constitution

of, or belonging to, the working class

a policy of preventing Soviet communism from spreading into new countries or states

a relaxation of tensions, especially between nations

a hit-and-run fighter

Name _____

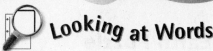

Predicting Meaning

The meaning of each root word of each vocabulary word below is given. Using the prefixes and word parts from the box, write your prediction of the meaning of each vocabulary word on the line next to the word.

in- or *im-*: in, into	*de-*: remove	*non-*: not
geo-: ground, earth	*multi-*: many	*hydro-*: water

1. *colonization:* establish a colony in a certain place

   decolonization:_____

2. *forestation:* the covering of an area with a forest

   deforestation:_____

3. *migration:* movement from one place to another

   immigration:_____

4. *renewable resource:* a natural resource that can be replaced

   nonrenewable resource:_____

5. *thermal energy:* power from hot springs or heat

   geothermal energy:_____

6. *electric energy:* power from electricity

   hydroelectric energy:_____

7. *ethnic nation:* a country based on one ethnic group

   multiethnic nation:_____

Combine the correct prefix or word part from the box with the root words below to build words that correctly complete the sentences.

8. *patient*   As an _____, the patient had to stay in the hospital.

9. *grain*   This _____ cereal has more than one grain.

10. *centric*   Something that is _____ relates to the center of the earth.

11. *phobia*   A phobia is a fear, and _____ is a fear of water.

12. *frost*   To get rid of frost, _____ the freezer.

13. *violent*   The _____ leader was never violent.

Notes for Home: Your child practiced predicting the meaning of this unit's vocabulary words. **Home Activity:** Explain to your child that *ex-*, *re-* and *uni-* are opposite in meaning to *in-* or *im-*, *de-*, and *multi-*, respectively. Have your child write pairs of words for each set of "opposites," such as *inhale* and *exhale*.

Name _____

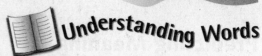

Earth Puzzle

Fill in the blanks of the puzzle with the vocabulary words that best complete each of
the sentences below. Solve the puzzle by finding the word spelled vertically by the letters
in the boxes.

1. _____ **energy** is produced from the energy of flowing water.

2. A _____ **resource** can be replaced.

3. _____ of resources prevents waste and is one solution to the energy crisis.

4. _____ occurs when topsoil dries and blows away due to farming
   and overgrazing.

5. _____ **energy** is produced from super-hot underground water.

6. _____ **fuel** is formed deep in the earth from plants and animals.

7. _____ gas is caused by the burning of gasoline.

8. Global _____ is explained by scientists using the greenhouse effect.

9. _____ occurs when trees are cleared from land and soil becomes less fertile.

10. The _____ **effect** is caused by an increase of #7 in the atmosphere.

11. _____ is the process of making the environment dirty.

1. __ __ __ __ __ __ __ __ __ __ __

2.   __ __ __ __ __ __ __ __ __

3. __ __ __ __ __ __ __ __ __

4. __ __ __ __ __ __ __ __ __ __

5. __ __ __ __ __ __ __ __

6.   __ __ __ __ __ __ __

7. __ __ __ __ __ __ __ __ __ __ __ __

8.   __ __ __ __ __ __ __

9. __ __ __ __ __ __ __ __ __ __ __

10.   __ __ __ __ __ __ __ __

11. __ __ __ __ __ __ __ __ __ __

These words are all about the: _____

Vocabulary Workbook

© Scott Foresman 6

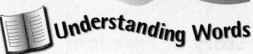

The End

Knowing suffixes can help you predict the meaning of new words. When you know the meaning of the base word and the meaning of the suffix, you can understand the new word. Look at the word *protection*:

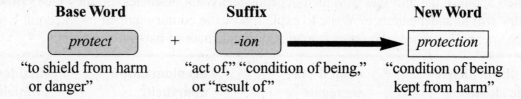

Base Word		**Suffix**		**New Word**
protect	+	*-ion*	→	*protection*
"to shield from harm or danger"		"act of," "condition of being," or "result of"		"condition of being kept from harm"

Each of the word families below includes a vocabulary word from this unit. For each, the base word has been defined. The box below gives the definitions for the suffixes that all of the words share. Using what you know about the definitions of the base words and the suffixes, predict the meanings of the words in each word family. Use a dictionary to check your answers.

-ion means "act of," "condition of being," or "result of"
-ism means "act or practice of," "quality of being," or "theory or doctrine"
-ist means "person who does or makes," "expert," or "person who believes in"
-ive means "of having to do with" or "likely to"

---

1. *repress:* to prevent from doing something

   repressive: _____

   repression: _____

2. *terror:* violence that causes fear

   terrorism: _____

   terrorist: _____

3. *environmental:* to hold back or restrain

   environmentalist: _____

   environmentalism: _____

4. *pollute:* to make the environment dirty

   pollution: _____

Notes for Home: Your child predicted the meaning of vocabulary words and related words by applying the meanings of base words and suffixes.
Home Activity: Ask your child to make a list of other words with the suffixes *-ion*, *-ism*, *-ist*, and *-ive*.

Story of Freedom
Expository Writing

Toward the end of the twentieth century—and in the beginning of the twenty-first century—
many countries were trying to gain their independence. Think about one of the countries that
you learned about in the unit that won its independence. What obstacles did they face? How did
the country win its independence? Write to explain how the country gained its freedom. Use at
least three vocabulary words. You may use an additional sheet of paper.

civil disobedience	coup d'état	decolonization	dissident
ethnic cleansing	segregate	apartheid	ethnicity
multiethnic nation	perestroika	repressive	terrorism
trade agreement	trading bloc	Zionism	glasnost

_____

_____

_____

_____

_____

_____

_____

_____

_____

_____

_____

_____

_____

_____

_____

_____

_____

_____

Notes for Home: Your child wrote an expository paragraph explaining how freedom was won
by a country in the late twentieth or early twenty-first century.
Home Activity: Invite your child to explain to you how another country won its independence.

decolonization

coup d'état

segregate

apartheid

sanction

civil disobedience

Zionism

dissident

perestroika

the overthrow of a government

the process of replacing colonial rule with self-rule

a system of laws in South Africa, which kept blacks and whites separate

to separate

the refusal to obey or cooperate with unjust laws

a penalty placed against a country to force it to change its ways or policies

a protestor against a government

a movement that began in the 1800s to set up a Jewish state in Palestine

"restructuring"; a reform movement introduced by Mikhail Gorbachev to restructure the Soviet economy

✂

glasnost	**gross domestic product (GDP)**
trading bloc	**euro**
trade agreement	**ethnicity**
multiethnic nation	**ethnic cleansing**

© Scott Foresman 6

a measure of a country's wealth

"openness," a policy introduced by Mikhail Gorbachev in 1985 to allow the Soviet people some freedom of speech

the money of the European Union

a group of nations that agrees to trade under favorable conditions

a group of people with the same language, customs, and culture

an agreement with rules about the exchange of goods between countries

to drive out or kill people who do not share the same ethnicity or identity

a nation with different ethnic groups living together

repressive

terrorism

millennium

megacity

demographer

immigration

zero population growth

global warming

the use of violence and fear to achieve political goals

something that restrains

a city region with more than 10 million people

a period of 1,000 years

to leave a home country and go to another country to stay permanently

a person who studies population trends

a gradual increase in the temperature of Earth's surface

the balance between new babies born and people lost due to death

carbon dioxide	greenhouse effect
pesticide	environmentalist
endangered species	deforestation
desertification	pollution

the process by which carbon dioxide in Earth's atmosphere traps heat from the sun, raising the temperature of Earth's surface

a gas produced by the burning of gasoline

a person who tries to solve environmental problems

a chemical that is used to kill insects

the clearing of land, which causes loss of forests and less fertile land

an animal or plant that is in danger of dying out completely

the process of making the environment dirty

the drying up of land along a desert

conservation	**fossil fuel**
nonrenewable resource	**renewable resource**
hydroelectric energy	**geothermal energy**
space station	**satellite**

a fuel formed long ago deep in the earth from prehistoric plants and animals

the use of resources carefully and wisely

a natural resource that can be replaced

a resource that cannot be replaced

energy that is produced from super-hot, underground water

electricity produced by using the energy of flowing water

an object that is sent into space and orbits Earth

a large, orbiting scientific base used by humans in space